MW00651408

BARBADOS

AN ISLAND PORTRAIT

BARBADOS

AN ISLAND PORTRAIT

Photographs by Mike Toy
Text by Peter Laurie

MACMILLAN
CARIBBEAN

Macmillan Education
Between Towns Road, Oxford OX4 3PP
A division of Macmillan Publishers Limited
Companies and representatives throughout the world

www.macmillan-caribbean.com

ISBN 978-0-333-94596-4

Text © Peter Laurie 2005
Photographs © Mike Toy 2005
Map © Macmillan Publishers Limited 2005

First published 2005

Designed by Mark Straughan at R.M.T. Photographics Ltd.
Map illustrated by Peter Harper
Cover design by Mark Straughan at R.M.T. Photographics Ltd.

The publisher and author wish to thank the following rights holders for the
use of copyright material: Mrs Frank Collymore for the extract from 'Hymn
to the Sea' and 'Triptych' by Frank Collymore; W M Foster for the untitled
poem by Michael Foster; Brian Forde for the extract from 'Heart of an Island'
by A N Forde

If any copyright holders have been omitted, please contact the publishers who
will make the necessary arrangements at the first opportunity.

Printed and bound in China

2009 2008 2007
10 9 8 7 6 5 4 3 2

CONTENTS

PREFACE

I've always thought it a good idea to carry a camera at all times. And never have. Just an old system in the car with a couple of lenses would do as you never know what you're going to see. I can't begin to count the number of times I've driven past something and thought 'that would make a lovely photograph and I don't have a camera.' But in trying to fill in the gaps for this book I realise that these things are here all the time, we just don't see them unless we decide to look. Thus in this respect the pictures in this book are nothing out of the ordinary but rather moments of what is everyday life in Barbados.

Much of the island has changed dramatically in the past fifteen years. New roads, golf courses, a marina and any amount of new villas and condominium developments. Being stuck in traffic can be an everyday occurrence; something that was unheard of ten years ago. We even have a rush hour. We have the Internet, satellite TV, international business parks, digital cameras and almost everyone has a mobile phone. Friends abroad find the rush hour bit hard to believe but we are, after all, listed by the UN as the world's foremost developing nation. Progress always comes with a price. And then there are things that have not changed at all. You can still be the only person on Morgan Lewis Beach, still see people washing clothes at a standpipe, still encounter donkey carts, still buy a coconut for a dollar and listen each night to a chorus of crickets and tree frogs.

Progress and development can change the nature and identity of a nation's people but Bajans are Bajans and will always remain uniquely so, development or not. I still cannot get used to the fact that wherever you go in this country complete strangers will always acknowledge your presence. Sometimes it's just a mumble or a nod of the head, others a fully-fledged 'Good morning.' It's one of my favourite daily experiences. Try looking a complete stranger in the eye in New York City and saying 'Good morning' or ending a telephone conversation with 'Have a blessed day.' You'd more than likely be thought a little strange.

To try and thank everyone individually who has made this book a reality would simply not be possible so instead I'd like to extend my thanks and appreciation to Bajans one and all. For their warmth and hospitality, directions, suggestions, historical insights and local information.

Page i: Symbol of the age when sugar was king, this derelict sugar windmill is now covered with a glorious bloom of Shower-of-Gold.

Pages ii - iii: Sunset on a west coast beach seen through a grove of graceful coconut trees.

Page iv: A costumed reveller at Kadooment, the popular carnival-like festival.

Pages v - vi: Kite surfing at Silver Sands, Christ Church.

Pages vii - viii: Contrasts of modernity and tradition. Part of the exterior of the ultra-modern Central Bank building (1980s). Dimly reflected in the glass are the clock tower of Parliament (1880s) and the national flag.

Page ix: One of the ubiquitous green monkeys of Barbados – apparently hitching a ride on a tortoise. The monkeys, which have encroached into residential areas, are best seen in their natural habitat at the Wildlife Reserve.

Page 3: A thundercloud drifts toward the setting sun off the west coast.

Page 4: Ragged Point Lighthouse, St. Philip. There are four lighthouses in Barbados, located at strategic points on the coast. The others are South Point in Christ Church, Needham's Point in St. Michael, and Harrison's Point in St. Lucy. The Ragged Point lighthouse was erected in 1875. The lighthouses are no longer operational.

N

Atlantic Ocean

North Point
Animal Flower Cave

Greenidge

Harrison
Point

Pie Corner

ST. LUCY

Gay's Cove
Pico Teneriffe

St. Lucy's

St. Nicholas
Abbey

Barbados
Wildlife
Reserve

Morgan
Lewis Mill

ST. PETER

Six Men's
Bay

Farley Hill
National Park

Signal Station at Grenade Hall

Scotland

St. Peter's

St. Andrew's

Long Pond

Speightstown

Belleplaine

ST. ANDREW

District

Turner's
Hall Wood

Cattlewash

Bathsheba

ST.
JOSEPH

Tent Bay
Andromeda Gardens

ST. JAMES

Flower
Forest

St. Joseph's

Portvale Sugar
Factory

ST. THOMAS

Cotton
Tower Hill

Hackleton's Cliff

Newcastle

Consett
Bay

Holetown

St. James'

St. Thomas'

Villa Nova

Bath

Codrington
College

St. John's

Harrison's Cave

Ragged
Point

Holder's
Hill

Fisher Pond
Plantation House

ST. JOHN

Warrens

Gun Hill Military
Signal Station

ST. PHILIP

Francia
House

ST.
GEORGE

Drax
Hall

St. Philip's

Bottom Bay

ST. MICHAEL

Sunbury House

St. George's

Six Cross Roads

Spring
Garden

Tyrol Cot
Heritage Village

National Stadium

Kensington Oval
Cricket Ground

River

Constitution

Bridgetown

CHRIST CHURCH

Cobbler's Reef

Carlisle Bay

Garrison

Needham's
Point

Graeme Hall
Swamp

Grantley Adams
International Airport

St. Ann's Fort

Worthing

Maxwell
Coast

Christ Church

Oistins

South Point

Caribbean Sea

Scale

0   1   2   3   4   km

0   1   2   3   4   miles

IN THE BEGINNING

Barbados… a flat disc of coral shivering in the still turning claws of the sea.

George Lamming, from *The Pleasures of Exile*

IN THE BEGINNING

The small island of Barbados, 'the Rock' as it is affectionately called by those who cling to it – 'cling' in both senses of love and anxiety – has long been recognised as a peculiar place that defies, if not description, at least explanation.

It is a place full of contradictions, ambiguities and subtleties that are often lost on the casual observer.

Geologically distinct from the neighbouring islands, which are largely of volcanic origin, the coral island of Barbados stands alone as the eastern sentinel of the Caribbean. Because of its geographical position – the first landfall from Europe – and historical economic importance – the sugar jewel in the eighteenth-century British Crown – Barbados became the military and administrative hub of the British West Indies.

The striking impression of Barbados is that of a small, flat, tidy island. Yet the majestic wildness of the blustery, rugged Atlantic coast to the east never fails to surprise the traveller journeying from the placid beauty of the Caribbean west coast.

Whereas other islands changed colonial hands like so many pieces of currency, Barbados remained, from its settlement in 1627 until its independence in 1966, a British possession. This gave Barbadians a sense of historical stability and continuity, and perhaps a certain smugness that can irritate the outsider. A parliament, set up in 1639 to serve a narrow set of interests, proved three centuries later to be an indispensable instrument of freedom and justice for all.

Pages 14 - 15: *Carlisle Bay, Bridgetown, named after James Hay, the first Earl of Carlisle, is the historic anchorage for ships calling at Barbados. After the building of a deep-water port in 1961, the bay is now used mainly by pleasure craft. It is bordered by one of the most beautiful beaches in the Caribbean.*

Above: *Inland landscape at Dunscombe, St. Thomas.*

Above: *Turner's Hall Wood in St. Andrew, the only area of original pre-settlement vegetation remaining in Barbados. Most of the island was deforested in the 17th century for cultivation of tobacco and cotton, and subsequently sugar cane. The wood, which encompasses about 74 acres, has over a hundred different flowering plants.*

The people of Barbados – the Bajans – out of a brutal history that pitted British planter against African slave, had the resilience and creativity to forge a unique Barbadian nation and to fashion a post-colonial society as famous for its political stability as for its economic viability. Barbados is, for all its tiny size and lack of resources, the leading developing country according to the United Nations Human Development Index.

Yet Barbadians now feel the strains of the global changes convulsing the world. How will they cope? While adapting, will they keep the strong sense of self that has served them so well in the past?

PAST IS PROLOGUE

I see these ancestors of ours:
The merchants, the adventurers, the youngest sons
of squires,
Leaving the city and the shires and the seaports,
…
I see these ancestors of ours
Torn from the hills and dales of their motherland,
Weeping, hoping in the mercy of time to return
To farm and holding, shuttle and loom
…
I see them, these ancestors of ours;
Children of the tribe, ignorant of their doom,
innocent
As cattle, bartered for, captured, beaten, penned
Cattle of the slave-ship, less than cattle.

Frank Collymore, from 'Triptych'

PAST IS PROLOGUE

Page 19: *The Emancipation Monument, sculpted by artist Karl Broodhagen, and erected in 1985 to commemorate the 150th anniversary of the emancipation of the slaves. The statue is sited at the roundabout at St. Barnabas, St Michael. The statue is popularly known as the 'Bussa statue' in memory of Bussa, National Hero and one of the leaders of the 1816 rebellion, the most important in the history of Barbados.*

Pages 20 - 21: *Central Bridgetown with Parliament on the right, the Careenage on the left, and National Heroes' Square in the centre with the 1882 Fountain Gardens in the foreground.*

Left: *Suazoid pottery head circa* AD *1200-1500, one of many Amerindian artefacts unearthed during the construction of the Port St. Charles marina.*

Barbadians have shown a reluctance to come to terms with their past, largely because much of it – the enslavement of Africans – was brutal. Misplaced sensitivities about past injustices suggest that we politely draw a discreet veil over the past and get on with the business of living. Yet the past not only explains the present but may even hold the key to the future.

How can you possibly explain the character of the Bajan today without recourse to history?

Our history has roots in the continents of Africa and Europe, from where our ancestors came, but it is a history forged unmistakably in the crucible of the Caribbean against the great historical sweep of the forces of conquest, genocide, exile, slavery and indenture.

Top: *Clay body-stamps used to apply dyes to the skin on ceremonial occasions.*

Bottom: *Blue-head wrasse carved from conch shell. The hardest material available to the Amerindians, conch was also used to make tools and weapons.*

24

Above: *Young sugar cane plants with a derelict windmill in the background. Sugar has lost its dominant place in the economy, and more Barbadians are now hoping for a sugar cane-growing industry with multiple by-products.*

Our history begins with the Amerindians, of whom there
now remains only an archaeological presence on the island.
The capital, Bridgetown, however, was named after a bridge the
Amerindians had erected over what is now the Constitution
River.

Barbados was home to these people who, at various periods,
came from the Orinoco region of South America up the island
chain. The Amerindians were mainly farmers and fishermen,
and traces of some fifty of their settlements have been found
around the coasts of the island, dating back to at least 2000 BC.

Above: *The famous bearded fig tree after which
Barbados was supposedly named by Portuguese sailors,
who thought the trees reminded them of bearded men*
(los barbudos) .

One Amerindian group gave the name Ichirouganaim – 'red land with white teeth' – to the island. The name probably referred to the red soil and the foam-covered coral reefs of the island. The name 'Barbados' was supposedly given to the island by Spanish or Portuguese sailors in reference to the hanging roots of the bearded fig trees that once grew widely here.

In 1500 there were estimated to be just above 8,000 Amerindians on the island. However, by the time the first eighty English colonists and ten African slaves arrived in 1627 it was uninhabited. The Amerindians had either been captured or killed by the Spanish or had moved elsewhere in the archipelago.

Above: The ruins of Farley Hill, one of the finest of Barbadian plantation houses, built in 1857 and gutted by fire in 1957. The grounds, which afford a magnificent view of the east coast, are now a national park and popular picnic site.

The colonists quickly began clearing the forests and planting tobacco, cotton, indigo and ginger, and by 1650, the crop that was to turn Barbados into the most prosperous of British colonies, sugar cane.

The British settlers quickly set about creating the beginnings of a society that was to incorporate throughout its history strong positive legacies such as the English language, the common law, religion, parliamentary government, sound systems of public administration and education (Codrington College in Barbados became in 1875 the Caribbean's first institution of higher learning), and, of course, cricket.

The settlers established a parliament in 1639 (the second oldest in the New World) to run their affairs, and in 1652, in the Charter of Barbados, wrested from the British the principle of no taxation without representation. This parliament was to form a thread of continuity throughout the history of Barbados.

Page 28: Statue of Lord Nelson, erected in 1813 to honour the admiral's famous victory at Trafalgar in 1805. The statue and its central location in the capital have become a bone of contention in the 'culture wars' of Barbados, between, on the one hand, those who argue that it is a symbol of British supremacy and an irritating reminder of a repressive colonial past and should be destroyed, and, on the other hand, those who wish to keep all symbols of 'little England' alive. Fortunately, the voices of the sensible majority, who believe that historical artefacts should be preserved in their proper place, have prevailed, and the statue is to be relocated to a naval museum to be created on a renovated pier head in Bridgetown.

Page 29: *Morgan Lewis Sugar Windmill in St. Andrew was the last windmill to operate. It closed in 1947. It was lovingly restored by the National Trust in 1999 and grinds sugar cane once a month during the harvest (February to July).*

Facing page: *The Barbados Mutual building in Broad Street, Bridgetown - an architectural gem dating from 1895.*

Above: *Streetscape of old Bridgetown featuring one of the typical cast iron balconies. Note also the Dutch gable of the building on the left.*

It proved in the first two centuries to be largely an instrument of the planters for remorselessly prosecuting their own interests, primarily against the slaves and free blacks, but also against the British Crown when necessary. By 1661 Barbados had a comprehensive slave code which accorded masters, servants and slaves carefully differentiated rights and obligations. Black property holders were excluded from the franchise by law in 1721 until the law was repealed in 1831.

British colonialism also left negative legacies in the form of an exploitative plantation economy, slavery, and, afterwards, oppressive conditions of life for most of the freed population, and a virulent white racism that characterised this society for most of its existence.

Yet with the broadening of the franchise in the nineteenth and twentieth centuries, culminating in universal adult suffrage in 1950, the same parliament became an instrument for bringing social and economic justice to the people through a peaceful social revolution.

It is this tradition of struggling for social justice through gradual parliamentary reform that underlies the famed political stability of Barbados today, with two main political parties, the Barbados Labour Party and the Democratic Labour Party, alternating in office.

The production of sugar beginning in the late 1640s dominated and shaped much of Barbados' history. It was the basis of an unprecedented prosperity, which, along with a strong resident settler class (23,000 by 1655), allowed commerce, arts and sciences to flourish to such an extent that when George Washington visited the island for three months in 1751 – at the height of sugar's dominance – Barbados and Boston were the two thriving commercial and intellectual centres of the English-speaking New World and Bridgetown would have been the largest city he had ever visited.

Pages 32 - 33: Barbados' Parliament, which has met without interruption since 1639, is the third oldest in the Commonwealth. The present buildings, housing the elected House of Assembly and the appointed Senate, were erected in the 1870s. The clock tower was built in 1884. Parliament is the central institution underlying Barbados' enduring political stability.

Above: Gun Hill Signal Station in St. George is the largest and most important of the six military signal stations that were set up across Barbados from 1818 to 1819. The stations were so situated that a signal, by either flag or semaphore, could be relayed quickly from one end of the island to the other. They were set up in the aftermath of the 1816 slave rebellion so as to warn the military authorities both of internal trouble and of possible attack from the sea by foreign forces. Gun Hill was also used as a convalescent post for military personnel.

It was sugar that made Barbados into the administrative, economic and military hub of the Caribbean. It was the headquarters of the British army (until 1905) and the navy (until 1805) in the eastern Caribbean.

Bridgetown became the most important port city in the entire British West Indies. A Roman Catholic priest, Father Labat, visiting Barbados in 1700, described the city as '... fine and noble; its streets are straight, long and clean and well intersected. The houses are well built in the English style with many glass windows; they are magnificently furnished. The shops and the merchants' warehouses are filled with all one could want from all parts of the world. One sees numerous goldsmiths, jewellers, clockmakers and other artificers ... ' One can only hope that the current plans for the redevelopment of Bridgetown will restore much of its lost glamour.

Above: Cannon at the Garrison Savannah in St. Michael – part of a splendid collection at this site. The oldest cannon is the Commonwealth Gun of 1660 with the Republican coat of arms on the barrel.

The heyday of sugar would come to an end in the middle of the twentieth century, but by then Barbados had discovered a new mainstay of the economy: tourism.

Sugar also shaped the very structure of the society and economy. It is a labour-intensive industry and indentured servitude was first tried, giving rise to the famous 'Redlegs' or poor whites of the eastern parishes of the island – and then African slavery.

In 1655 there were 23,000 whites and 20,000 slaves. In 1712 there were 12,528 whites and 41,970 slaves. And by 1829 there were 14,959 whites, 82,802 slaves and 5,146 freedmen.

Between 1640 and the end of the slave trade in 1807 nearly 400,000 Africans were brought to Barbados as slaves. The history of Barbados is largely the history of their oppression, their resistance and struggle for freedom, and their creation of new forms of social and cultural expression.

One of the most famous slave revolts in Barbadian history was the 1816 armed rebellion associated with the National Hero, Bussa. (Barbados has ten 'National Heroes', created by legislation in 1998 – individuals who have made an outstanding contribution to the history or culture of Barbados.) The 1816

Above: Codrington College in St. John, the oldest institution of tertiary education in the West Indies, functioning as a theological college preparing candidates for the Anglican ministry since the 1870s, affiliated first to the University of Durham from 1875 to 1955 and more recently to the University of the West Indies. The college was built in 1745 on the grounds of the ancestral property of Christopher Codrington, a Barbadian planter who left his estates in Barbados to educational and charitable purposes. Codrington also left his books - and money to build a library - to All Souls College, Oxford. The site of Codrington College is a magnificent one with beautiful grounds and an ornamental lake.

Above: *Portvale Factory in St. James, one of only two sugar factories still working. From the early 17th century sugar was made in wind-powered mills, until the introduction of steam-driven factories in the late 19th century. As part of the ongoing rationalisation of the sugar industry over the past few decades, most of the factories across the island have been closed. Whether sugar production will survive far into this century is questionable, but certainly not as an industry geared to the export of raw sugar in bulk.*

rebellion was influenced by the 1804 Haitian Revolution as well as by the growing debate in England over the immorality of slavery.

Although the rebellion was crushed, the spirit of resistance lived on.

The rebellion led to some improvement in the treatment accorded to slaves, but also to a tightening of the internal security arrangements, such as the erection in 1818-19 across the island of a number of military signal stations, the most famous of which is Gun Hill in St. George.

Emancipation in 1834 formally ended slavery in Barbados, but the political, social and economic condition of black Barbadians continued to be deplorable. A number of laws were passed after Emancipation to control the free black workers in the interests of the white property-owning classes.

The spirit of revolt that characterised the 1816 rebellion was to be seen in the life of another National Hero, Samuel Jackman Prescod, one of the leading political figures of the nineteenth century who, as the leader of the free blacks before Emancipation in 1834, struggled unremittingly for the rights of the masses afterwards. In 1843 he became the first black Member of Parliament.

It was the political linkage between the outstanding leaders of the small black middle class and the working class that would prove critical to stable progress. Dr Charles Duncan O'Neal, the son of a black planter, was another middle-class black Barbadian who, in the early twentieth century, worked on behalf of the masses.

The experiences of black Barbadians in the First World War, and of those 20,000 who had emigrated to help build the Panama Canal, coupled with the writings of black nationalists like Marcus Garvey, all helped to ferment discontent in the stifling social and political atmosphere of Barbados in that era.

O'Neal founded the Democratic League in 1924 and the Workingmen's Association in 1925. He was a Member of Parliament from 1932 until his death in 1936. He, too, is a National Hero.

But it was the National Rebellion of 1937 that was to usher in the greatest period of change in our history and chart the course for independence.

The 1937 rebellion was sparked by the deportation of National Hero Clement Payne, a Trinidad-born political agitator who had been holding hugely popular meetings in protest at the intolerable social and economic conditions in which the vast majority of Barbadians lived.

In the 1930s, the condition of the people throughout the British Caribbean colonies was deplorable. It was a time bomb waiting to explode. Payne's deportation was the spark that ignited the rebellion in Barbados. Beginning on the 26th July, the people rose up, primarily in the capital, but also throughout the island. The rebellion lasted four days. Fourteen people were killed, forty-seven wounded and four hundred arrested, before order was restored.

The 1937 National Rebellion was to lead to the creation of mass-based political parties and trade unions, the extension of the franchise, and a host of legislation that improved life for the majority of Barbadians.
Following universal adult suffrage in 1950, Barbadians gained ministerial self-government in 1954; suffered the sad, failed experiment of a West Indies Federation from 1958 to 1962; and then won independence in 1966.

The outstanding figure of this progressive period in our history was Grantley Adams, who emerged after the National Rebellion in 1937 as the political leader *par excellence* of both the Barbados

Labour Party (BLP) and the Barbados Workers' Union. He became the premier of Barbados in 1954, and then the prime minister of the ill-fated Federation in 1958. Adams' political genius allowed him to wrest political power from the planters and merchants without wrecking the economy. He was the father of our democracy. He is also a National Hero.

Two other brilliant figures from this period were Hugh Springer and Frank Walcott (National Heroes), the organisational genii who more than anyone else helped mould the strong, united trade union movement that is responsible for much of the stability and the prosperity that Barbadians enjoy today.

The person who had the responsibility for leading Barbados into independence and guiding the country for a decade after was another political genius, Errol Barrow. This National Hero had broken away from the BLP in 1955 to form the Democratic Labour Party (DLP). He succeeded in laying the basis of a modern Barbadian economy and society, and spreading the wealth of the country more equitably without causing the predominantly white business community to flee the country in the first uncertain years of independence.

Above: The lion at Gun Hill was carved by Henry Wilkinson, the Adjutant-General of the Imperial Forces stationed here in 1868. Etched into the base of the limestone sculpture is the carver's name, rank and completion date of the work. There is also a Latin inscription that translates as 'It shall rule from the rivers to the sea, and from the sea to the ends of the earth.'

Between them, Adams and Barrow took the country from the stark polarisation of a wealthy privileged few confronting a dispossessed working class to a modern liberal social democracy. They expanded the economic base of the society and, through free education, health services and affordable housing, enlarged the middle class. Between them they created – with a little bit of luck – a deep-rooted two-party political system.

Left: *The Main Guard at the Garrison, St. Michael. St. Ann's Garrison was the headquarters for the British forces in the West Indies from 1870. The Garrison was created around the 18th-century St. Ann's Fort, incorporating a large parade ground (the Savannah – now a horse race track and sports ground and site of an impressive collection of ancient cannon), barracks and residences, a military prison and hospital and other buildings including the Main Guard with its splendid clock tower. The entire complex is one of the outstanding colonial garrisons in the world. St. Ann's Fort is now the headquarters of the Barbados Defence Force.*

Above: *Hurricane shelter at Fisher Pond Plantation House.*

Both of them, in their different ways, were 'evolutionaries' rather than revolutionaries. They knew how to use their mass support to good effect to achieve the reforms they wanted; but they also knew how and when to strike sensible compromises. They were masters of the art of the possible.

Subsequent leaders have built on their achievements.

The Barbadian business community has also evolved from the reactionary, racist planter-merchant oligarchy of the 1930s into one of the most enlightened and responsible corporate sectors.

Nothing reflects the political genius of the Barbadian people for consensus and compromise so much as the present 'Social Partnership' that brings together government, business community and trade unions in pursuit of national productivity, prosperity and equity.

Out of a difficult history Barbadians have, against all the odds, managed to forge a post-colonial polity, economy and society that works and is often referred to internationally as 'the Barbados Model'.

LANDSCAPE / SEASCAPE

Always, always the encircling sea,
eternal: lazylapping, crisscrossed with stillness;
Or windruffed, aglitter with gold…
Her lullaby, her singing, her moaning; on sand,
On shingle, on breakwater, and on rock;
By sunlight, starlight, moonlight, darkness:
I must always be remembering the sea.

Frank Collymore, from 'Hymn to the Sea'

LANDSCAPE / SEASCAPE

Page 43: *Sunset on the west coast.*

Pages 44 - 45: *Pico Teneriffe, St. Peter. This prominent landmark on the east coast was named after a presumed resemblance to a peak of the same name in the Canary Islands.*

Top left: *Aerial view of the St. James coastline, the 'gold coast.'*

Bottom left: *Dusk falls at Needham's Point, St. Michael.*

Landscape is a powerful force in shaping the people of a country.

It is impossible to conceive of the Bajan without conjuring up an image of this flat, tidy little island where nature, if not entirely tamed, is at least civilised to the point where it is in harmony with human settlement.

This is evidenced in the care that Barbadians lavish on the land; both the plantation house and the modest little chattel house will have a lovingly tended garden.

Barbados is a coral island. The oldest parts of it emerged out of the sea some 600,000 years ago. Most of the island's surface is coralline, but the Scotland District to the east is an area where the coral cap has been lost, exposing the underlying oceanic deposits. The coralline structure has also created some fascinating caves with stalactites and stalagmites, the most famous of which is Harrison's Cave in St. Thomas, in the centre of the island.

47

Pages 48 - 49: *Harrison's Cave in St. Thomas - the most spectacular of the caves in the centre of the island, created by underground streams. The cave, with its large chambers, waterfalls and pools, is one natural attraction that should not be missed.*

Pages 50 - 51: *A cliff and land-locked stack at Pie Corner, St. Lucy.*

Top left: *Sugar cane fields at Black Bess, St. Peter.*

Bottom left: *Root crops such as yams and sweet potatoes have been a traditional part of Barbadian agriculture.*

Above: *Natural erosion has resulted in the formation of these sculpted 'hoodoos' at Morgan Lewis in the Scotland District, St. Andrew.*

The relatively flat nature of the island, rising gradually from the south and west in a series of terraces to the highlands of the central and eastern parishes of St. George, St. Thomas, St. John and St. Joseph, also facilitated the creation of an extensive network of roads and the almost complete cultivation of the land.

The small fields of sugar cane and vegetables such as corn, yams and sweet potatoes that cover the countryside – interspersed with rows of cabbage palms and groves of mahogany trees – are a dominant feature of the landscape. It is a patchwork of gentle greens and mild browns, to be seen to best effect after the harvesting of the sugar cane in the second quarter of the year, especially in the St. George Valley.

Above: *The rolling hills of the Scotland District in St. Andrew with Morgan Lewis Mill to the left.*

54

Above: *Egrets nesting in Graeme Hall Swamp, Christ Church. This is one of the few surviving mangrove swamps that once were common along the south and west coasts. Graeme Hall, which encompasses about 90 acres, is now a major bird and nature sanctuary.*

The mangrove swamps that originally stretched along much of the south and west coasts are now confined to one area – Graeme Hall Swamp, a sanctuary for birds.

The small size and accessible nature of the island encouraged an abiding sense of community, however torn at times by tensions.

Pages 56 - 57: *A magnificent view of the wind-swept east coast.*

Top left: *Long Pond in St. Andrew on the east coast. Fed by streams from the hills of St. Andrew, Long Pond is the largest inland body of water after Graeme Hall Swamp.*

Bottom left: *Stormy weather approaching the east coast. An average of ten tropical storms reach the Caribbean each year. Originating off the west coast of Africa, six will develop into hurricanes; two of these will be major.*

Above: *A chattel house nestled on the slopes below Hackleton's Cliff, an escarpment that runs from St. John's church to Cotton Tower Hill in St. Joseph, close to 1,000 feet above sea level.*

The lack of resources in the earth, the very thinness of the soil itself in many places – in just scraping the earth you often touch rock – induced habits of husbandry and instilled in the Barbadian prudence and caution.

The gullies of Barbados offer a glimpse of the original forested nature of the island as well as of its only wild mammal, the ubiquitous green monkey. Landscaped gardens like Andromeda and the Flower Forest are rich in tropical trees, shrubs and plants.

Pages 60 - 61: *Barbados is home to over 700 species of flowering plants although few are indigenous.*

Above: *Bottom Bay, St. Philip.*

The landscape in Barbados, while picturesque, is not one that inspires awe. There are no huge mountains, vast valleys, or immense forests.

It is a landscape in which you sense that neither has man vanquished nature nor that nature threatens to overwhelm man. You get the impression that a sensible bargain has been struck; as Frank Collymore put it in one of his poems, 'a land of pastel tints and compromise'.

The nearest you get to grandeur in the landscape of Barbados is the east coast, its rugged coastline and beaches blasted by the salt-laden wind and pounded relentlessly by the surf of the Atlantic Ocean. The majestic sweep of that boulder-strewn coast rising up to the hills and cliffs above it has little in common with the quiet tropical charm of the palm-fringed white beaches of the west coast.

Above: *Steps cut into the rock provide access to the beach at Enterprise, Christ Church.*

Above: *The relentless pounding of the Atlantic surf on the rugged cliffs of the north coast.*

The landscape is dotted with the presence of history. There are military forts (St. Ann's Fort and the Garrison have a world-famous collection of seventeenth-century English cannon), signal stations and outposts that the British set up from as early as the seventeenth century in this Caribbean headquarters of their navy and army. One also sees the relics of the stone sugar mills (with a restored fully functioning one at Morgan Lewis in St. Andrew), the great houses of the plantocracy and the architecturally unique chattel houses.

Then there is the sea, always the sea. Barbadians have a deep love and inordinate respect for the sea. It is a brave Barbadian who will break an ancient taboo to venture into the sea on Good Friday. Any Barbadian who has lost a loved one to the sea will tell you that 'the sea has no back door', or, when it is particularly rough, that 'the sea is calling', that is, seeking a human sacrifice. It is also from the sea that come the dreaded hurricanes that visit our shores every fifty years or so.

Above: *Gibbs Beach, St. Peter.*

Right: *Walking the beach at Bathsheba, St. Joseph.*

Facing page: Top left: *Snorkelling above a wreck in Carlisle Bay.*
Top right: *Maxwell Beach on the south coast.*

Bottom: *The 'soup bowl' at Bathsheba – surfers' paradise.*

Above: *Tent Bay at Bathsheba – a traditional fishing village.*

Top left: *Fishing boats at Tent Bay.*

Bottom left: *Cast-netting at Mullins Beach, St. Peter.*

Above: *Surfers enjoying the remnants of the day.*

At the same time we earn our livelihood from the sea, whether through fishing or tourism.
The sea and the beach are also our places of recreation. Older Barbadians believe that a sea bath, especially early in the morning, has the power to restore and make whole.

Indeed, Barbadians seem to draw psychic strength from the encircling sea.

ALL GOD'S CHILDREN

The indigenous Carib and Arawak Indians, living by their own lights long before the European adventure, gradually disappear in a blind, wild forest of blood. That mischievous gift, the sugar cane, is introduced, and a fantastic human migration moves to the New World of the Caribbean: deported crooks and criminals, defeated soldiers and Royalist gentlemen fleeing from Europe, slaves from the West Coast of Africa, East Indians, Chinese, Corsicans, and Portuguese. The list is always incomplete, but they all move and meet on an unfamiliar soil, in a violent rhythm of race and religion. Today their descendants exist in an unpredictable and infinite range of custom and endeavour, people in the most haphazard combinations, surrounded by memories of splendour and misery, the sad and dying kingdom of Sugar, a future full of promises.

George Lamming, from *The Pleasures of Exile*

ALL GOD'S CHILDREN

Page 73: *Our future.*

Pages 74 - 75: *Bajan portraits.*

Left: *Kadooment reveller.*

George Lamming's description above of the peopling of the Caribbean applies with one important difference to Barbados. After the abolition of slavery in 1834, because the whole island was already under cultivation as plantations or small farms, there was no hinterland to which the former slaves could go to make a living as peasants. They were therefore forced to work for subsistence wages on the plantations. Hence there was no need to import indentured labour from India and China, as happened in Guyana and Trinidad.

The original Amerindian people of the island have long gone, leaving only remnants of their way of life – pottery, ornaments, tools and one rock carving in Springhead Cave in St. James – from their more than one hundred settlements around the island. They have also given us words like barbecue, hammock and hurricane. The English settlers also adapted one of their rituals – impaling pineapples on sticks at an entrance to ward off evil spirits – by using stone pineapples as finials on gateposts.

Pages 78 - 79: *Relaxing at the beach, Carlisle Bay.*

Left: *Boy at standpipe. The public standpipe (short for standard pipe – introduced in 1861) was once the major source of water for many households and a place where people congregated and exchanged gossip. Now, with practically every home supplied with water, the standpipe is a vanishing icon of old Barbados.*

Above: *Cane cutter in the cane field. Today the sugar cane is mainly harvested mechanically.*

Apart from the Amerindians, everyone else in Barbados comes from somewhere else. The vast majority came from the Senegambia region of West Africa as slaves, enduring the nightmare of the Middle Passage.

The others came mainly from Britain as farmers, adventurers, prisoners of war, convicts and indentured servants, some of whose descendants, known as the 'Redlegs', still live on the eastern side of the island where the soil is poorest. This motley group of British emigrants was what Professor Richard Burton has referred to as 'the deracinated, the deranged, the debauched, and the desperate'.

The fact that we are a nation of emigrants has had a contradictory impact on Barbadians, as it has had on other peoples of the New World.

On the one hand, it has led to an undercurrent of rootlessness and uncertainty about national identity, accompanied by occasional calls for a loyalty to ancestral homelands. In this scenario, Barbadians are part of someone else's diaspora.

But it has also fostered, through creolisation, such national traits as adaptability, creativity and a quickness of mind and spirit that allows the Barbadian, like other Caribbean people, not only to survive but also to prosper in the most trying circumstances. In this scenario, Barbadians create their own diaspora.

One of the symbolic figures of this creativity and determination is London Bourne, who was born a slave in 1793, was freed when he was 25 years old, and went on to become, against all odds, one of the richest merchants in Barbados, a sugar broker and the owner of two plantations. He was an active supporter and friend of Samuel Jackman Prescod.

The Barbadians traditionally to be found in other Caribbean islands were invariably policemen, teachers and preachers, which says a lot about Barbadian life: in a small crowded space, order and discipline are essential requirements.

Above: *Roadside coconut vendor in Holetown, St. James.*

Facing page: Top left: *Corn vendor on the ABC Highway. Locally grown, the corn is roasted on old-fashioned coal pots (also known as Dutch ovens).*
Top right: *A fisherman checks his nets for flying fish – some 1.5 million are caught in local waters each year and are one of the island's most popular delicacies.*

Bottom right: *Typical produce of a market vendor: pumpkin, sweet potato, yam, cassava, christophene and tomatoes.*

Cricket and carnival, two fundamental elements of play in the Caribbean, are prime examples of the creolising spirit taking customs imported from other societies and transforming them into unique expressions of Caribbean culture. Who else but a Caribbean people – the Trinidadians – would have taken discarded oil drums and fashioned one of the most original and subtle musical instruments of the twentieth century: the steel pan?

Page 84: Top Left: *Postman.*
Top right: *Car washer.*

Bottom: *Barber.*

Page 85: *Island constable.*

Above left: *A family dressed for church, Boscobelle, St. Peter.*
Above right: *Family and friends.*

Facing page: Top left: *Father and daughter.*
Top right: *Father and son.*

Bottom: *Children playing in the shallows at Bathsheba, St. Joseph.*

Of course, while Barbadians share a Caribbean culture, they put their own peculiar stamp on it, a stamp that derives much from their own history (an unbroken colonial association with England and the first landfall for slaves from Africa), geography (a community created by the necessity of living cheek by jowl in a small space, whatever the tensions created by gross inequalities in wealth and power), and a God-fearingness (for want of a better word) that finds expression in many outlets.

This results in a personality that can sometimes smack of overweening national pride.

The Barbadian is often viewed by other Caribbean people as somewhat conservative, somewhat stodgy, somewhat sly, somewhat frugal and very full of himself.

Above left: *Cooling out.*
Above right: *Sunning.*

Above: *Monkeying around on Kadooment day*.

When President Bill Clinton chose Barbados as the site for the historic US-Caribbean summit in 1996, a Caribbean person was quoted in *The New York Times* as saying that it was the logical choice for a well-organised and safe meeting, and then added with a delicate touch of mischief, 'besides, they're going to work, not have fun.'

Other outsiders have been harsher in their judgements. The Welsh socialist, Gordon Lewis, in his *The Growth of the Modern West Indies*, begins his chapter on Barbados with the memorably malicious words, 'It is difficult to speak of Barbados except in mockingly derisory terms.' He also refers to Bajans as 'stiff with starch and Anglicanism'.

The Barbadian does indeed have a strong sense of
self – a psychic centre around which all the elements of his
complex personality cohere. Even if the Barbadian travels to
the ends of the earth – and he has – he takes his Barbadianness
with him, like the character Pig-Pen in the Peanuts comic strip
who has this permanent and impenetrable cloud of dust
hovering around him.

This personality is reflected traditionally in a fierce individual
drive to succeed through self-reliance, hard work, thrift and
shrewdness, with a high premium placed on education and
ownership of property. Owning a 'house spot' is still one of the
cherished ambitions of most Bajans.

Yet this individualism is more often than not tempered with a
strong sense of obligation to the community, with compassion
for the disadvantaged and the less fortunate, and with love of
neighbour. The folk institution of the Friendly Society and the
custom of the 'meeting turn' (an arrangement between a group
of people for compulsory saving/interest free loans), along with
a vibrant credit union movement and an extensive social
security system, reflect these values.

Above: *Daybreak at Tent Bay, St. Joseph.*

Above: *Spring Garden on Kadooment day.*
Kadooment - a Barbadian term meaning a 'big
occasion' - is the culmination of the Crop Over
festival which runs from June to the beginning
of August and celebrates the end of the sugar
cane harvest. Kadooment, held on the first
Monday in August, involves dozens of
masquerade bands with thousands of costumed
revellers dancing in the streets. It starts at the
National Stadium and ends on the Spring
Garden Highway, next to the cooling sea. It is
one of the greatest street parties in the
Caribbean.

The Bajan also has a love of freedom tempered by respect for law and tradition, an insistence on the right of self-government and a commitment to settling one's differences by peaceful discussion. You can experience this spirit in any rum shop, or by listening to the radio call-in programmes.

Barbadians rebelled violently in 1816 and 1937, because they saw no other way out of the repressive social order of the times. But elections in Barbados today, although vigorously contested, are peaceful and orderly affairs. Barbadians are evolutionaries rather than revolutionaries.
They are at heart a peaceful, tolerant and friendly people.

GUARDIANS OF OUR HERITAGE / CRAFTSMEN OF OUR FATE

The old sugar mill today a mass of broken
Stone is also a monument of the living poem
of people
Who gave to life with lips shut tight to staunch a scream,
And died knowing their blood was changing
the colour and
Character of the soil and their breath was not idle.
…

But there is a consolation: each year
clanging on time's anvil
Brings nearer conqueror and conquered:
the moon can teach
The sun the merit of a soft light. Nor is
the conqueror
A stranger always: for a man can be his own
conqueror
His skin may fall about him like a sack
or like a robe
Adorn him.

A.N. Forde, from 'Heart of an Island'

GUARDIANS OF OUR HERITAGE / CRAFTSMEN OF OUR FATE

Page 93: *Calypsonian John King.*

Pages 94 - 95: *Masqueraders at the National Stadium on Kadooment Day.*

Left: *This masquerader in all her finery is caught up in the musical fervour of Kadooment.*

To appreciate the culture of Barbados you have to understand two things: the origins of that culture have roots both in Africa and Britain, but the resulting fusion is uniquely Caribbean.

While Britain provided the formal institutional framework – language, law, church, education, etc. – within which Barbadians lived their culture, Africa provided the underlying substance, so that how we pray, play, love, eat and drink, talk, tell jokes, dance and make music, render the world in our arts and view life, are all profoundly influenced by our African roots, regardless of the colour of our skins or the place of origin of our ancestors.

Top left: *'Slamming dominoes' – one of the favourite pastimes in rum shops. The rum shop is a unique popular watering hole and gathering place for relaxed and unrefined enjoyment.*

Bottom left: *Rum shop on Bay Street, St. Michael. So how do you tell a rum shop from a regular bar? The best answer is that you know you're in a rum shop:*

When you order rum by the bottle and not the glass;
When the ice comes in a plastic container;
When you drink beer from the bottle;
When nobody is sipping a glass of wine;
When there is no waiter service;
When there are foodstuffs on the shelves behind the bar;
When everybody is talking at the top of their voices;
When dominoes are being loudly slammed in the background; Or something like that. Cheers!

Above: *The drum corps of the band of the Royal Barbados Police Force.*

The culture the Africans brought with them was usually suppressed by force or driven aside by the colonial authorities. But it was not lost. The enslaved Africans had the courage, the resilience and the strength of character to resist the most dehumanising conditions of life, and in the interstices of that bleak wasteland, had the creativity and imagination to fashion a world of their own.

The African culture, based on a deep respect for nature in which the world of spirits was always immanent, flourished underground to spring up again in new and enriched forms, or peeped out in the cultural activities of the dominant European class, as a visible strain that was no longer alien, but a fundamental part of a creole Caribbean culture that is the product of many influences.

The essence of creolisation is its resilience and wonderful capacity to adapt and adjust, its inventiveness and sheer imaginative genius. All these qualities are evident in so much of Barbadian, as in Caribbean, life: in our food, religion, music, literature, painting, dance, games, and above all in our language.

Creolisation was clearly evident from the early eighteenth century, facilitated by the small size of the community and the ease of communication.

The Barbadian language – Bajan – is a fine example of creolisation. It is a variant of English that has been influenced by the syntax, sounds and rhythms of West African languages, and that has developed to interpret the unique Barbadian social and physical environment. Several expressions in Bajan either come from Africa – like the common 'wunnah' (you plural) – or from seventeenth-century English – like 'primpler' (prickle or thorn).

Several visitors to the island in the eighteenth century observed disapprovingly that the whites spoke in 'the Negro style'.

Above: *The Barbados Defence Force's band in their colourful Zouave uniforms, originally worn in the French colonial service and then subsequently by the West India Regiment from the 1850s. The uniform is named after a Berber people from Algeria.*

Top right: *The Barbados Landship, an icon of Bajan folk culture, does one of its intricate 'naval' manoeuvres outside the hallowed precincts of Parliament.*

Bottom right: *The Landship doing a manoeuvre, known as the Maypole. This involves plaiting and unplaiting long coloured ribbons around the pole while dancing to the infectious rhythm of a tuk band. The men are dressed as naval officers and the women as nurses. The look may be English, but the movements are definitely African. The Landship is a form of working class friendly society and a typical example of Afro-European fusion.*

There is a beautiful economy to Bajan, as in expressions like 'she step out to come back' or 'when you miss me I gone', which convey a wealth of meaning in a few words.

You can find the magnificent use of Bajan language in the writing of Barbadian poets like Kamau Brathwaite, and novelists such as George Lamming and Austin 'Tom' Clarke. The latter's *Pigtails 'n Breadfruit* is an indispensable and entertaining introduction to Bajan language and food. Frank Collymore's little book, *Barbadian Dialect*, is a useful and amusing guide.

Since independence, there has been ferment in, and flourishing of, the arts in Barbados. This is only natural. A people must find its own voice – that is, a way of seeing the world that is unique and a way of expressing what it sees that is unique; in other words, a way of asserting its unique cultural identity.

Page 102: *Fire eater.*

Page 103: *The Mighty Gabby, Barbados' foremost calypsonian and folk singer. His poignant and haunting 'Emmerton' is one of the greatest folk songs in the world.*

Above: *Stilt men and shaggy bears, two traditional folk dancers performing to the music of a tuk band.*

Above: *Tuk band with saxophone player. The tuk band is derived from the British fife and drum bands transformed by African rhythms – yet another example of the creolisation that typifies Bajan culture.*

While this holds true for all peoples, it is all the more important for a colonised people to reclaim its own reality from the coloniser, because, as the great Irish novelist James Joyce put it, 'my soul frets in the shadow of his language'.

This does not mean repudiating the past or 'revising' history in the sense of ignoring unpleasant facts or even inventing fanciful interpretations. It means seeing and interpreting what was and is significant for us who dwell in the Caribbean, rather than for those who dwell in Europe.

We have, however, not only to rescue our past for ourselves from the competing distortions of colonialism, but also to lay claim to our future against the cultural globalisation that threatens to overwhelm us.

105

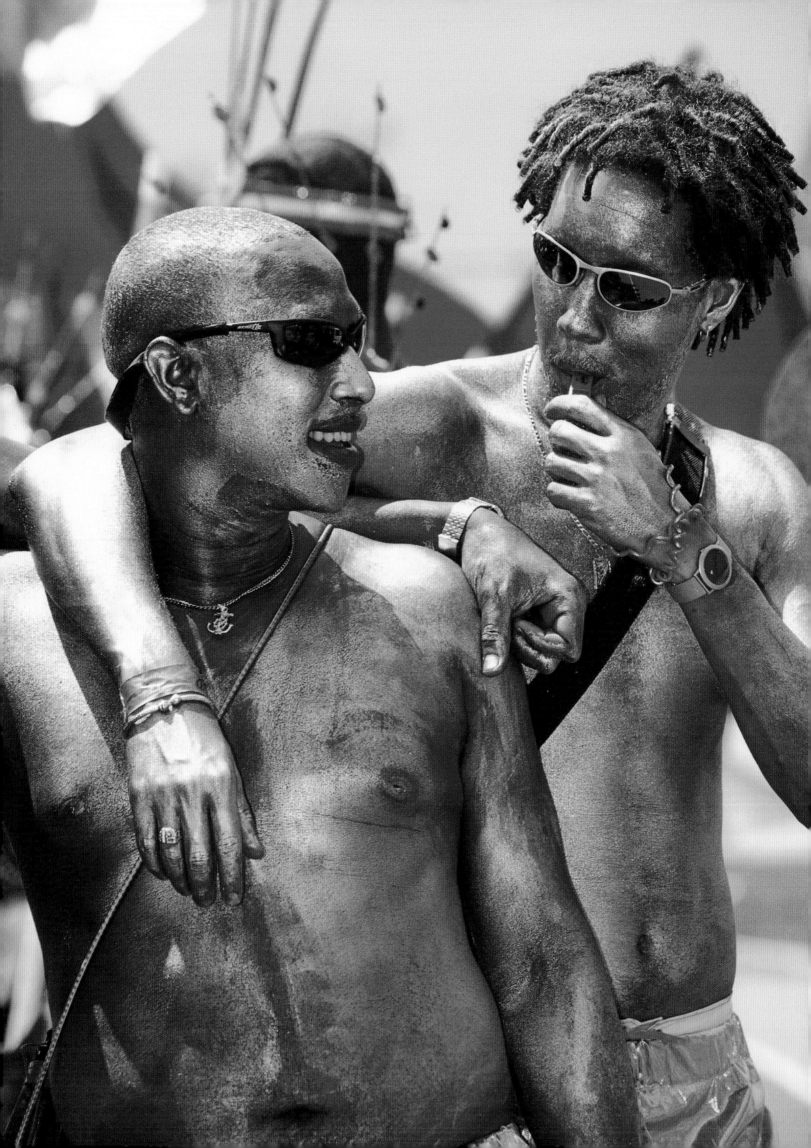

It is in this sense that cultural development is the finding of our national 'voice'. It is our artists who give us this national cultural voice. The writers, painters, musicians, singers, dancers, architects and other artists who render and shape our reality in an aesthetic form that not only gives us pleasure but helps us to understand and interpret the world for ourselves.

The literary godfather of Barbados is Frank Collymore, who edited the journal *BIM* for decades, starting in the 1940s, and nourished the talents of a host of Caribbean writers including our foremost novelist, George Lamming, and our unofficial poet laureate, Kamau Brathwaite. John Wickham, like his father, Clennel, a distinguished man of letters, was the last editor of this famous journal.

Pages 106 - 111: *Revelling at Kadooment.*

Left: *Seeking directions?*

Above: *A masquerade band makes its way down Brighton Road to Spring Garden Highway on Kadooment Day.*

The National Cultural Foundation, established in 1984, has played an indispensable role in stimulating the arts.

It has taken pains to help keep alive traditional aspects of Barbadian culture, such as the Landship (another creolised fusion of European and African elements; the Landship is a fraternal organisation that allowed the poor to pool their savings; it recreates the camaraderie and discipline of the navy, but on land, and with a distinctly Caribbean musical and dance flavour; the Landship parades in public, performing British naval routines to African rhythms); tuk bands (yet another felicitous example of creolisation whereby the European fife and drum band is radically transformed by African musical patterns); stilt walking; the game of warri; sticklicking (an ancient martial art that originated in Africa); steel pan; calypso; and the foremost Barbadian festival, Crop Over, which celebrates in music and dance the end of the sugar cane harvest, climaxing with the spectacular carnival parade, Kadooment, on the Spring Garden Highway on the first Monday in August.

Above left: *Arturo Tappin, Barbados' pre-eminent saxophonist, with an international following.*

Above right: *Saxophonist working the crowd at the Holetown Festival. Held in mid-February each year the festival commemorates the landing of the island's first colonial settlers at Holetown in 1627.*

Above: The late Karl Broodhagen, a great artist and sculptor – creator of the Emancipation Monument, and along with his son Virgil Broodhagen, of statues of National Heroes Sir Grantley Adams and Sir Garfield Sobers.

Other aspects of traditional culture, like the rum shop, with its dominoes, draughts and free-flowing conversation, survive on their own as a testimony to their social indispensability.

The NCF has also helped facilitate new expressions of the artistic spirit through its festival competitions, like the National Independence Festival of Creative Arts, and the provision of necessary arts infrastructure.

Indeed, largely due to the promotional efforts of the NCF, Barbadian music has flourished to such an extent that it has become a major export. Singers, like Gabby, Allison Hinds, Red Plastic Bag, John King, and Edwin, musicians, like Arturo Tappin and Nicholas Branker, and many other *artistes* have built strong international reputations, following in the footsteps of pioneers like Jackie Opel and the Merrymen.

Painting, sculpture and ceramics have also made great strides with the consolidation of the reputation of established artists like Alison Chapman-Andrews, Joyce Daniel, Karl Broodhagen, Fielding Babb, Goldie Spieler, Courtney Devonish and Roger Moore, and the emergence of a plethora of younger artists, some of whom, like Ras Akyem and Ras Ishi, are already establishing serious international reputations. The number of art galleries that have sprung up and the host of exhibitions held are testimony to the dynamism in these art forms.

Barbados has a fine architectural tradition dating back to the seventeenth century, as evidenced by the Jacobean masterpieces St. Nicholas Abbey and Drax Hall, as well as later structures such as Sunbury, Villa Nova and Francia House.

Top left: *St. Nicholas Abbey in St. Peter. A superb specimen of a Jacobean great house, dating from the 1650s. Note the elegant Dutch gables.*

Bottom left: *The 'Trinidadian House' in Worthing, Christ Church, so called because of its ornate style.*

Above: *Fisher Pond Plantation House.*

Building styles, based on English models, evolved over the years to incorporate features that suited the climate, environment and national sensibility. The Barbados National Trust has played an essential role in conserving and restoring some of our best specimens of traditional architecture.

The chattel house is a cultural icon of Barbados that illustrates the wedding of beauty to necessity. The freed slaves were allowed to build houses on plantation property, but they had to be movable and were therefore known as 'chattels', which means 'movable possessions'. They were designed as modular structures that could easily be assembled, disassembled, and transported to another location on the back of an ox-cart or, more recently, a flatbed truck. Apart from the functionality of the chattel house, it is its aesthetic details that have given it its unique appearance: hipped roofs, window hoods, wooden jalousies, ornamental fretwork, and distinctive pedimented porches and galleries.

Photography and video are arts that have also developed and flourished in Barbados, featuring many artists with strong international reputations.

Then there is food and drink; glorious, delicious food and drink. You can have your choice of fried, grilled or steamed flying fish, breadfruit, cornmeal cou cou, pudding and souse, pumpkin fritters, conkies, okras, yams, eddoes, sweet potatoes or hundreds of other mouth-watering local delicacies. And, lest we forget, Barbados is the home of rum, the best you can get in the world, from young light rums that mix well, to dark, aged premium rums that can be sipped like a cognac.

Now, that is artistry!

GIVE PRAISE, CHILDREN,
GIVE PRAISE

In the beginning
was no beginning,
for endless everything
always was.
Never being, but always being.
From nowhere,
From everywhere –
A silent nothing
Swelling forth
From ever…
to ever…
forever…

Michael Foster, from an untitled poem

GIVE PRAISE, CHILDREN, GIVE PRAISE

Page 123: *A beautiful stained glass window in St. Patrick's Roman Catholic Cathedral in Bridgetown. The present church dates from 1899.*

Pages 124 - 125: *Women attending a service at St. James' Anglican parish church on Mothering Sunday.*

Left: *Spiritual Baptist ceremony at the Apostolic Cathedral in Ealing Grove, Christ Church. Known locally as 'tie-heads' the Spiritual Baptists represent a true 'home-grown' indigenous religion.*

There are probably more religions or denominations of religions in Barbados than anywhere else in the world. Christianity in its many manifestations, Islam, Judaism, Hinduism, Bahai, Rastafari and a host of other religious expressions. And then, of course, there is cricket.

You find churches everywhere throughout the island, from stately stone Anglican edifices with stained glass windows, to tiny wooden structures that house only dozens of the faithful. In fact, for every rum shop you'll find a church, so that you could truly say that Barbados is an island of the spirituous and the spiritual.

Within a few years of arriving on the island, the early settlers divided the island into parishes, ten of them named after Christian saints, and one called Christ Church, and erected Anglican churches in each parish, starting with St. James' Church in Holetown and St. Mary's Church and St. Michael's Cathedral in Bridgetown. The parish churches of St. James and St. John are especially beautiful.

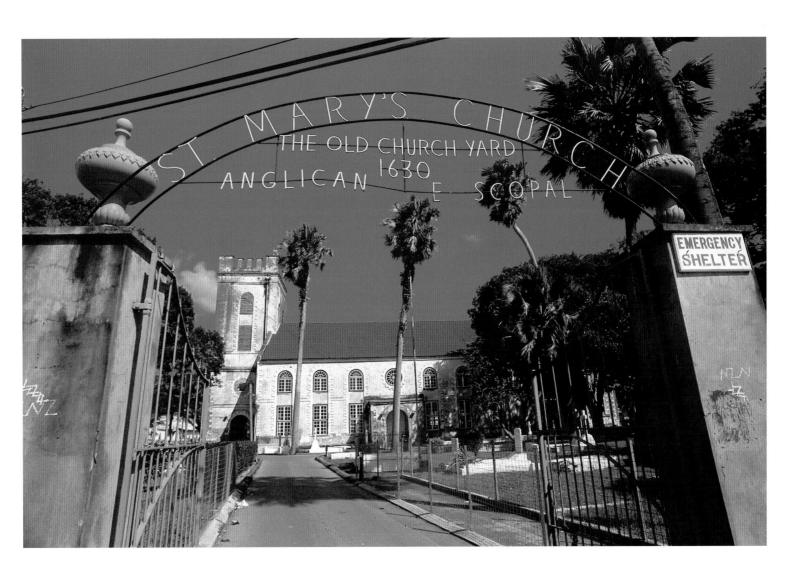

Pages 128 - 129: *St. John's Anglican parish church, one of the most beautiful of Gothic churches in Barbados, dating from 1836, has a magnificently carved pulpit. The church, sited on the edge of Hackleton's Cliff, commands a superb view over the east coast.*

Top left: *Small 'wayside' church, which speaks of the propensity of Barbadians to embrace religion in all shapes and sizes.*

Bottom left: *St. Margaret's Anglican church.*

Above: *St. Mary's Anglican church in the heart of Bridgetown. Built in the 1820s, it is a splendid example of a Georgian-style church.*

The Anglican Church was, from the Settlement, the dominant religion in Barbados, playing important social and political roles. The parish vestries were responsible for local government.

The Quakers were among the early settlers and accounted for almost a third of the population of Bridgetown by the 1680s. But partly because of emigration to Pennsylvania, and partly because they were persecuted for their opposition to slavery and to military service, their numbers dwindled.

Anglicanism remained the dominant religion throughout most of Barbadian history, and today still commands the allegiance of a third of the population, while the Pentecostal churches (a rapidly growing group), the Methodists, the Seventh Day Adventists, the Roman Catholics, the Moravians, and other denominations share the remaining Christian adherents. One of these thriving sects is the Spiritual Baptist Church, founded in 1957. It has strong African associations evident in its music, dancing, processions and rituals.

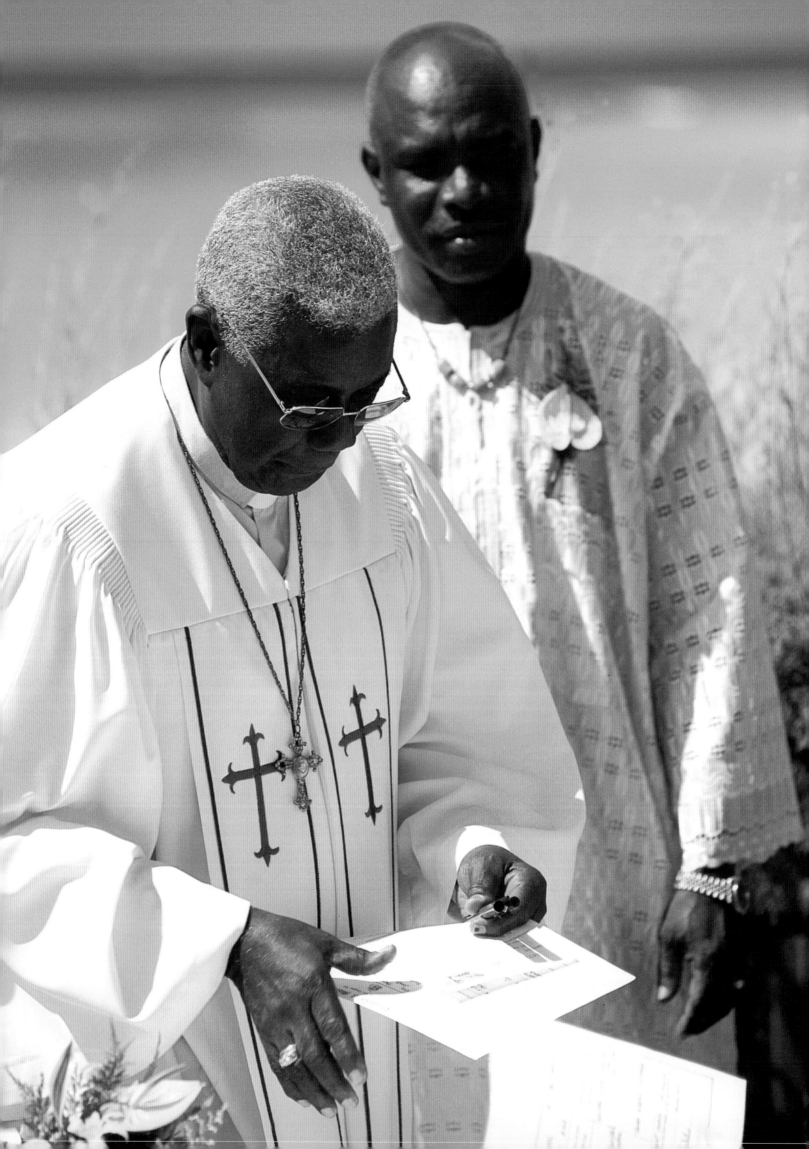

Pages 132 - 133: *From the conventional to the unconventional, Barbadians have always made great preachers.*

Left: *A service in St. James' Anglican parish church.*

Above: *The Jewish Synagogue in Bridgetown, established in 1654 to cater to a thriving Jewish community that had fled to Barbados from Spain and Portugal via Brazil. The present building was erected in 1833 to replace the original destroyed in the 1831 hurricane. The synagogue was refurbished in the 1980s. It is a beautiful blend of Jewish, Gothic, Renaissance and Barbadian architectural designs.*

There is a small Rastafarian community which also has its roots in Africa, as well as the religions of Islam and Judaism.

Indeed, the sizeable Jewish community that came from Brazil in the 1640s and 1650s, bringing with it the technology of making sugar, erected a synagogue in Bridgetown around 1660, one of the two earliest in the hemisphere. It was destroyed in the 1831 hurricane and rebuilt in 1833. By the end of the nineteenth century, however, most of the Jews had emigrated. The synagogue was sold in 1929 for use as an office building. But it was lovingly restored in 1983 by the new post-Second World War Jewish community, and is today one of the historical and beautiful buildings of Bridgetown.

While the early settlers were predominantly Anglican, the Africans who arrived from the middle of the seventeenth century to work as slaves on the plantations brought with them their own religions, beliefs and practices. These were based on a polytheism that saw a strong connection between the world of spirits and the world of nature, with special veneration towards one's ancestors. But these religious beliefs and practices were often suppressed by the colonial authorities, who also refused to allow the slaves to be converted to the Anglican religion.

Left: *Baptism at the seashore.*

Above: *St. Patrick's Roman Catholic Cathedral.*

The Moravians and the Methodists, whose arrival in Barbados coincided with the growing anti-slavery struggle, were often persecuted. One of the leaders of the Methodist community was National Hero Sarah Ann Gill, a free black woman who was relentlessly threatened and persecuted for her missionary activities. Her offer of a plot of land in James Street in Bridgetown in 1824 marks the origin of the James Street Methodist Church.

The Moravians also ran afoul of the authorities by reaching out to the slaves. In 1834 they established a congregation among slaves and ex-slaves in Bridgetown, and in 1849 the Calvary Moravian Church was built in Roebuck Street.

While, in Barbados, there is no equivalent of Haitian Voodoo or Cuban Santería, which are essentially African religions with a Catholic overlay, there is still a strong underlying Afro-Caribbean sensibility in the various forms of religious expression. This is perhaps best seen in the Spiritual Baptist Church, but can also be found to a lesser degree in other Christian sects, in the emotion, the singing, the dancing, the ritual and often in the possession by the Spirit.

Pages 138 - 139: *St. Lawrence Anglican church.*

Left: *St. Michael's Anglican Cathedral, built in the 1660s as the parish church and designated as the cathedral in 1825.*

Above: *The Chase vault in the cemetery of Christ Church parish church. This family burial vault has achieved notoriety because of strange happenings in it in the early 19th century. When the vault was opened in 1812 for the burial of Thomas Chase, the lead coffins within were in total disarray. They were rearranged. But when the vault was opened four years later for another family burial the coffins were once again out of place. This time sand was sprinkled on the floor to detect footprints and the vault sealed with cement. A few months later the seal was broken to admit another coffin and the coffins within were in even greater disorder. This occurred again, until the family directed that the all the coffins be removed and buried. Since then the vault has remained unused and the mystery unsolved.*

Barbadians of whatever faith can truly be said to be a God-fearing people. Not just church-going, though they are famous for that propensity, nor pious, a trait not normally associated with Barbadians; but God-fearing in the sense of having an unshakeable belief in a deity who has created this world for a purpose and by that mere fact commands obedience and humility.

Indeed, it is this recognition that they play an assigned role, however small, in a wider purpose, however mysterious, that nourishes the sense of self that allows Barbadians to face the future calmly, confident that if they look after the smaller things, God will look after the larger ones.

CRICKET, LOVELY CRICKET

ZAMAMA

ASIT ALI

WASIM

KHAN

NAZIR

An investigation of Worrell, Walcott and Weekes would tell us as much about the past and future of the people of the West Indies as about cricket.

C.L.R. James, from *Beyond a Boundary*

CRICKET, LOVELY CRICKET

Page 143: *Beach cricket, an ever popular activity. Cricket in Barbados is more of a religion than a sport.*

Pages 144 - 145: *Scoreboard at Kensington Oval, one of the great cricket grounds in the West Indies.*

Left: *Fervent English supporter at Kensington.*

To talk about sport in Barbados is to talk about cricket. And Bajans do talk about cricket – endlessly, over and over again, *ad nauseam*. Just go into a rum shop or anywhere that people congregate, or listen to the radio call-in programmes, and you will always hear someone holding forth on the subject of cricket.

And if the West Indies team is playing in a Test match, you will find Barbadians with their ears glued to the radio.

Indeed, some would argue that cricket in Barbados is less a sport than a religion. The Barbadian writer, John Wickham, has suggested that you might conceive of the field as a church, the spectators as the congregation, and the two wickets as a pair of altars, with the umpires as the officiating priests.

Left: *Two stands at Kensington Oval.*

Above: *West Indies vs England at Kensington Oval.*

Barbadians have a passion for cricket that surpasses all understanding. It is as if the game were fashioned to suit the Barbadian personality with its love of order and discipline within which great acts of heroic individualism are allowed to occur.

Bajan pride in cricket is justifiable. This tiny island has produced some of the greatest talent to grace a cricket field: from the pre-War era, George Challenor, considered one of the finest batsmen of his time, along with the great fast bowlers, Mannie Martindale and Herman Griffith; the famous trio of magnificent batsmen from the 1950s, Clyde Walcott, Everton Weekes and Frank Worrell, arguably the greatest captain of the West Indies team; the greatest all-rounder in the history of the game, the Right Excellent Sir Garfield Sobers; three of the finest West Indies opening batsmen, Sir Conrad Hunte, Gordon Greenidge and Desmond Haynes; along with some superb fast bowlers such as Wes Hall, Charlie Griffith, Malcolm Marshall and Joel Garner. This is just to mention a few.

It is no coincidence that Barbados' most popular National Hero is Sir Garfield Sobers. Barbadian historian Professor Keith Sandiford has pointed out that Barbados has for a long time been governed by two addictions: education and cricket. So powerful are these impulses that Barbadians have never been able to disentangle them. This obsession with cricket and education sometimes transcended matters of class and race in a community that was otherwise notoriously ridden with race and class prejudice.

But cricket is not the only sport practised in Barbados. Indeed, there are now so many sports played across the island that some people fear that cricket may be on the decline.

Barbados has produced a world-class sprinter in Obadele Thompson, winner of the bronze medal in the 100-metre event at the 2000 Olympics.

Pages 154 - 155: *Cricket at Trents, St. James.*

Left: *Polo at Holder's Hill.*

Above: *'Blast of Storm' wins the Sandy Lane Gold Cup at the Garrison Savannah.*

Barbadians have also successfully competed internationally at surfing and windsurfing, two very popular sporting activities.

Barbados has given the world a new sport, road tennis, a highly popular game usually played in the road as the name suggests, combining aspects of lawn and table tennis.

Page 158: Top: *Motor racing at Vaucluse in St. Thomas.*

Bottom: *Rugby at the Garrison Savannah.*

Page 159: *Out of the rough? Barbados boasts three championship golf courses: Barbados Golf Club, Sandy Lane and Royal Westmoreland.*

Pages 160 - 161: *Surfers off the cement plant in St. Lucy.*

Above: *Yacht racing in Carlisle Bay.*

Among indoor games, Barbados has produced a world champion in draughts. Suki King has taken on the world's best and beaten them at this ancient and highly popular game. There are also chess, dominoes, whist and bridge clubs.

Whether you're a Bajan or a visitor you can enjoy tennis, squash, polo, golf, volleyball, basketball, gymnastics, motor rallying, soccer, netball, horse racing, cross-country and distance running, cycling, archery, clay target shooting, field hockey, and an endless variety of water sports including diving, sailing, and game fishing.

Above: *Beach football.*

UPWARD AND ONWARD...
INSPIRED, EXULTING, FREE

We in the West Indies can meet the [future] without fear; for we begin with colossal advantages. The West Indian, though provincial, is perhaps the most cosmopolitan man in the world. No Indian from India, no European, no African can adjust with greater ease and naturalness to new situations than the West Indian.

George Lamming, from *The Pleasures of Exile*

UPWARD AND ONWARD... INSPIRED, EXULTING, FREE

Page 165: *The clock tower of Parliament.*

Pages 166 - 167: *View of the Royal Bank of Canada. Financial services play a leading role in the modern economy.*

Left: *The Central Bank building.*

So what does the future hold for 'the Rock' and the people who cling to it?

Modernity, like elsewhere, has been very much a mixed blessing. Its impact has swept away many of the traditional cultural habits of Barbadians. Moonlight nights in the country are no longer a time for telling stories on the front steps, or playing hop scotch, kick-the-tot pan or jacks in the yard. Television and Nintendo are more likely to be the occupation of children today.

Yet we ought not to romanticise poverty. Barbadians are far better off today than fifty years ago, with the provision of modern amenities in their homes such as electricity, running water, and telephones, and vastly improved systems of social security, health, transportation, housing and education.

These improvements to the quality of life have created the social capital which has pushed Barbados to the top of the list of developing countries in terms that take into account not only physical factors but also the human aspects of development.

The money that has financed this spectacular rise in living standards has come from the two most dynamic sectors of the economy: tourism and international financial and information services. Barbados is one of the most popular upmarket destinations in the world.

Tourism has benefited from a first-class port and airport and a healthy indigenous hospitality sector that includes hotels, restaurants and a variety of organised tours. But the key to tourism's success in Barbados is that it is not an enclave industry but one that is fully integrated into the landscape and lives of all Barbadians. Visitors to Barbados experience Barbados as it is, not as an all-inclusive fantasy.

Above: *Chattel houses in the city.*

Since the 1980s Barbados has become a world-class reputable financial and information services centre, linked by a network of tax treaties to the major industrial countries, and catering to banks, trusts, foreign sales corporations, exempt insurance companies, shipping registers, international business companies, and software development and informatics businesses.

Since tourism and international business services have never enjoyed any protection, these sectors are well equipped to take part in the new liberalised global economy.

Yet the challenges facing the country are serious: rising levels of crime and violence, drug abuse, HIV/AIDS, pollution of the environment, traffic congestion, and a worrying prevalence of chronic diseases like heart ailments and diabetes that stem from bad diet and lack of exercise.

Above: Broad Street, the main shopping street of Bridgetown.

Admittedly these problems are not peculiar to Barbados, but in a community that is so small they are particularly worrisome.

In addition, Barbados is a small and highly vulnerable economy in a world engulfed in the throes of radical changes that we have come to know as globalisation. While the services sector is well placed to compete globally, agriculture (especially sugar) and manufacturing face an uncertain future.

Barbadians, an evolutionary people, long accustomed to a process of slow, orderly change, are now confronted with a global chasm of progress that can only be crossed in one determined leap.

Pages 172 - 173: *The now defunct Hayman's Sugar Factory in St. Peter.*

Above: *Commercial complex at Warrens, St. Michael.*

Right: *The expanding private sector forms a vital part of the modern Barbadian economy.*

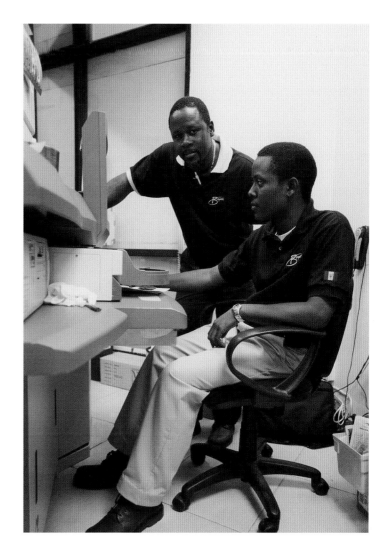

Barbadians, a conservative people, are now being invited to modernise their constitution, cast off the last vestiges of colonialism and take full responsibility for themselves as a republic with a Barbadian head of state, and with the highest court of appeal being a Caribbean Court of Justice rather than the Judicial Committee of the Privy Council of the House of Lords.

Barbadians, an insular people, are now being asked to merge their peculiar island identity in the wider identity of a Caribbean Single Market and Economy.

Can Barbadians use the courage and wisdom so typical of their forefathers to take the country forward into the new millennium?

Pages 176 - 177: *The Bridgetown port, one of the most efficient in the Caribbean, hosts numerous cruise ships.*

Above: *Lifeguard station.*

178

To do so, it will be essential for Barbadians of all generations, classes and races to unleash their full potential and make a wholehearted commitment to building a more prosperous, peaceful and equitable Barbados.

Barbados – the Rock – has all it takes to continue to prosper internationally, but in doing so it must not lose its soul.

We must become globally competitive, but we have to do it in the Bajan way.

Above: One in, one out. A departing cruise ship and approaching freighter.

179

Day Break on the East Coast

First light scours the furrows
Of ancient memories slashed in sand;
Scattering night's fleeting mysteries along the beach.

Salt-laden gusts scud along the coast,
Ruffling wisps of nightmares clinging to dunes,
Dispersing the dark and the dead.

Ghost crabs, scavenging for scraps of meaning
In hieroglyphs etched by the night wind,
Scuttle into holes.

The rustling of manacled bones in the surf ceases.
The blood-salted sea subsides.

Eternal baptism of light blesses the Rock-
Ichirouganaim: 'red land with white teeth'.

Snapshots.
A solitary cyclist, work-bound, pedals against the wind.
Monday morning face fixed in frown.
Two bathers brave shock of sea.
Shiver with renewal.
Shrieks of glee.

The village awakes. Voices across palings.
Sounds of frying. Smell of bakes.
Tea.

Children totter yawning from shuttered houses,
Book bags slung on backs for daily trek.

A packed, belching bus,
Climbs
the
long
winding
road
to
town.

The sun, cock-a-hoop, bursts out of the sea,
casting wide its net of light,
Restoring certitude and colour to the land.

Men find purpose;
Women strength;
Children delight.
Day breaks the hold of night.
Order is restored.
And so on.
And so on.
And so on.

Above: *Inter-island schooner 'Ecstasy'. Built in the 1920s she and others like her were the mainstay of trade among the islands of the Eastern Caribbean.*